LOCAL STUDIES LIBRARIES

Library Association Guidelines for Local Studies Provision in Public Libraries

D1742303

The Library Association

London

© The Library Association 1990

Published by
Library Association Publishing Ltd
7 Ridgmount Street
London WC1E 7AE

First published 1990

British Library Cataloguing in Publication Data

Library Association *Local Studies Group*
    Local studies libraries : Library Association guidelines
    for local studies provision in public libraries.
    1. Local history collections. Administration
    I. Title
    026.941

    ISBN 1-85604-005-4

Typeset in 12/13pt Palacio by Library Association Publishing Ltd
Printed and made in Great Britain by Amber (Printwork) Ltd,
Harpenden, Herts.

CONTENTS

FOREWORD

In the autumn of 1985 the Library Association Local Studies Group appointed a working party to prepare guidelines for the collection and care of local studies material in libraries. The working party consisted of Patrick Baird (Birmingham City Libraries), Don Martin (Strathkelvin District Libraries) and Tom Scragg (Knowsley Library Services), under the chairmanship of Diana Winterbotham (Lancashire Library); its recommendations have been adopted by the Local Studies Group after full consultation with the Group membership. The guidelines have been formulated with regard to public rather than special or academic libraries, but it is hoped that, as they contain much of a general nature regarding the use of local studies material, they will be helpful to librarians working in local studies collections of all kinds.

Many people have provided information and comment during the preparation of the guidelines; especially valuable was material collected by an earlier Local Studies Group working party convened in 1977 under the chairmanship of Harold Nichols. To that working party, to colleagues in Northern Ireland who gave generously of their time and expertise to comment on the draft report, and to all who have given their advice and support, the Local Studies Group offers sincere thanks.

Diana Winterbotham
March 1990

INTRODUCTION

1 Local studies: a definition

The term 'Local Studies', as applied to library local studies collections, can be defined as studies relating to the local environment in all its aspects, including geology, palaeontology, climatology and natural history; also as studies relating to all types of human endeavour within that environment, past, present and future.

2 Resources for local studies

It is essential to recognize that local studies researchers require resources which will facilitate the study of local subjects in the greatest detail possible. Material required will be not only printed items but also manuscripts, three-dimensional material, works of art, and minutiae and ephemera of all kinds.

The collection, custodianship and exploitation of such materials falls within not only the discipline of librarianship, but also the disciplines of museum curatorship and archive administration, each of which requires special training and skills. It is important to recognize that the complexity of the situation necessitates full cooperation between the respective professional staffs.

3 Collecting local studies material

It is essential that a collecting policy is formulated by the custodians of local collections. The policy should take into account other collections containing similar material (e.g. museum collections, archive repositories), and full discussions should be held with the professional staff supervising such collections. This is essential in order that (a) collections are not competing for material and unnecessarily duplicating holdings, and (b) the user does not have to visit several collections to find material which should be housed together.

The collecting policy should define (a) the topographical scope of the collection, and (b) the forms of material to be collected.

Local studies material is often rare and sometimes unique. Conservation is of prime importance in the administration of such material, as without adequate conservation its long-term use will be endangered. The holding of local studies collections implies a commitment to provide approved storage conditions and suitably qualified staff. It is important that the advice of professional staff in other disciplines is sought in appropriate cases, and if desirable for the care of the material, redirection to a more suitable repository (e.g. record office, museum) should be made.

Care of the material in the best available conditions should be of prime importance: neither local nor professional pride should be allowed to cloud the underlying issue.

Subject to the requirements of conservation implied above, convenience to the user is of great importance. Libraries have a particular commitment to ease of use by the public, in that they open for long hours, are often conveniently situated, have catalogues and indexes that may be easily consulted, and have good seating accommodation and access to facilities such as photocopying machines. Therefore, provided that the criteria for conservation can be met, the library is an ideal location for local studies material.

Funding must be sufficient to provide adequate staff, equipment, accommodation, books and local studies material of all kinds. Arrangements should be made to ensure that adequate contingency funding is available to purchase special items of local interest which appear on the market from time to time. A new local studies collection will require special funding during the early years of growth.

4 Bookstock

Printed books and pamphlets form the core of library local studies collections, and should be extensively collected and conserved. Multiple copies should be acquired in order to ensure adequate resources for present and future needs. Antiquarian booklists and shops should be actively searched in order to acquire out of print titles. Gift and exchange systems, both national and local, should be developed and encouraged, as this is a significant method of improving local studies collections; individual direct offering of material between libraries should also be practised. Staff should be aware of new opportunities for bibliographical searching offered by technological developments in bibliography, for instance the use of online services to identify periodical articles relating to local events. Publishing societies of local or regional importance (e.g. record societies, parish register societies) should be supported by subscriptions or grants as generously as resources allow, as such societies are a future source of published information, usually of a very high standard. All library staff should be trained to be alert to the identification of relevant locally published material.

In addition to specifically historical and geographical material, relevant current publications of all kinds should be sought, including all local authority publications. Other bodies which often produce important materials are churches, schools, political organizations, and local industrial and commercial firms; this list will be extended depending on local circumstances. Most local authority publishing is uncoordinated, and active seeking of this material from its various sources is essential. Appropriate general reference tools, bibliographies, and guides to the methods used in local studies should also be available in collections.

In addition to collecting material about the locality, many local studies libraries collect works by authors associated with the area, regardless of subject matter. In some cases the influence of the author's local background on a creative work is fairly easy to determine, in others less so, while in many instances the link between the author and the locality can be extremely tenuous. Care should therefore be taken to establish criteria by which the works of local authors are acquired for comprehensive or selective representation.

Some local studies collections incorporate special collections with significance beyond the boundaries of the local area (e.g. collections of material relating to authors of national reputation). The Local Studies Librarian should be alert to the need to publicize such material to potentially interested users outside the local area.

Modern reprographic methods (such as microform and photocopy) should be used to provide items not obtainable in hard copy: reprographic copies can also be used to save wear and tear on rare items. Adequate microform equipment should be provided for these uses.

Whilst it is recognized that the main part of the local studies collection will be a reference collection, many readers find it very convenient to be able to borrow books for home use, and a collection available for home reading is likely to be appreciated by many readers who would be unwilling or unable to undertake serious research on library premises. Loan collections of the most useful and popular books, both current and out of print, should be built up as quickly and widely as funds and the available material permit. The loan collection should be administered either directly or indirectly by the Local Studies Librarian.

In some cases libraries hold collections to which only limited access can be allowed (for instance, collections which hold sensitive material of recent date) or collections which are physically inaccessible, in an outstore. Care should be taken to ensure that catalogues contain sufficient information to avoid such collections being overlooked by the researcher, and to make sure that they are made as fully available as confidentiality and the conditions of deposit allow.

5 Newspapers and periodicals

Locally published newspapers are of prime importance and should be collected exhaustively. Indexes, which greatly enhance the use of local newspapers, should be compiled wherever possible. In addition to newspapers, other local journals should be collected, including journals and newsletters of local societies; parish, school and college magazines; house journals of local firms; commercial and industrial newsletters; and newsletters of bodies such as local community councils.

Periodicals dealing with the techniques of local history and archaeology should be represented in the collection, e.g. periodicals such as *Local historian* and *Local history*.

The collection should be supplemented by copies of relevant articles in periodicals and newspapers not otherwise added to library stock. It is essential that staff working in other library departments are alerted to identify local material in the stock of those departments, and to inform the Local Studies Librarian of items identified.

Collections of news cuttings are important in the local studies library even when a complete run of a newspaper is held and indexed. Cuttings provide ready dossiers of information for researchers which can easily be photocopied, and can also provide a convenient source of material for exhibition purposes.

6 Ephemera

Selection policy should include ephemeral material such as trade catalogues, programmes for local events, annual reports of local organizations, posters, timetables, sale catalogues, election publicity and other political material, catalogues of local exhibitions, and publicity material issued by local firms.

7 Maps and plans

Ordnance Survey maps. Collections should include all

11

maps published for the defined area at scales of 1:10 000/6" to 1 mile and larger. It is recognized that for libraries with large rural coverage this will not usually be immediately possible, but a gradual and methodical programme of completing collections by modern reprographic methods should be undertaken, subject to the restrictions of the Copyright Acts. Newly published maps on the above scales should all be purchased as published. Smaller scale Ordnance Survey maps should also be sufficiently represented in the collection to meet the needs of researchers; in some collections this may imply comprehensive coverage as with the larger scales.

Local Studies Librarians should be aware of the modern methods of updating Ordnance Survey maps (SUSI and SIM) and should take steps to ensure that such revisions are adequately represented in the library stock.

Other maps. Non-Ordnance Survey maps of all scales and dates should be comprehensively collected, including modern street maps.

8 Illustrations

Photographs. Photographic collections form an important part of library local studies collections, and are heavily used for many purposes. It should be recognized that other collections, especially museum collections, also have photographic material, and there should be cooperation between the relevant collections to develop policies for the acquisition, storage and public accessibility of photographic illustrations. Postcard collections may or may not be integrated with other photographic collections, but the above principles apply.

It is desirable that every photograph should be copied and a copy made available for day-to-day use, and the negative filed separately from the print. Although this may not be achievable in the short term in the case of large collections, such a policy will overcome many difficulties of damage and theft. Negatives should be acquired wherever possible, and always when a photograph is commissioned (i.e. the negative should not be filed at the photographer's studio).

The black and white negative is still generally regarded as the most stable form of archival photographic record and should be used as the main corpus of the collection. Original photographic prints should also be held as part of the archival record, and care taken that appropriate storage facilities are provided for their conservation.

Full details relating to a photograph should be recorded separately from the print on acquisition, including identification of the subject of the photograph, its date, donor or other source of acquisition, and whether copyright restrictions apply. If the negative number is added to this record, it can prove useful if any prints are lost or damaged, and can also be used for indexing purposes.

Colour prints and slides are a useful supplement to photographic collections. Whilst a colour slide is less convenient than a print for library use, it is the most economical form of colour record and the quality is technically superior to that of a colour print. Moreover, a collection of colour slides is an important educational aid, and can also be valuable for use in publicizing the local studies library.

Library photographic collections should always include coverage of the present day scene. Towards this end Local Studies Librarians should organize photographic surveys of local scenes and events. An awareness of local redevelopment schemes is essential in order to enable 'rescue' photography to be undertaken effectively. Whilst much record work will be carried out by the library or a paid agent, it is sometimes the case that a local photographic society is a willing helper; provided that steps are taken to ensure that the archival quality of the processing is to a satisfactory standard, such links should be welcomed both on financial and community grounds. Aerial photographs should be acquired as extensively as funds allow; although they are usually expensive they are vital in some areas of historical research.

If a library photographic service is fully developed, it may become desirable and feasible to establish a photographic department with professional staff, equipment and darkroom facilities. An in-house department of this kind can be of great benefit in ensuring security of items being copied, in facilitating the making of copies for display purposes, and in implementing a planned programme of record work such as that outlined above.

Prints and engravings form a valuable part of the library's illustrations collection, and should be actively acquired, subject to cooordination with other local collecting bodies such as a local art gallery.

Original drawings and water colours. These may be more appropriately housed in the relevant art gallery: a collection policy in this respect should be agreed with the repositories concerned. Consideration should be given to acquiring colour slides or other copies of relevant works of art, for instance topographical paintings.

9 Recordings

Public use of all recordings, whether sound or visual, should always be from a copy and not the original. If local sound or film archive repositories are available, advantage should be taken of any storage facilities in which originals can be deposited, the library having copies made for library use. Libraries should always take full advantage of cooperation with specialist organizations such as sound and film archives, which are a valuable source of expertise and can often provide specialist services.

Adequate cataloguing of film and video material is essential, as the form of the material precludes adequate access in any other way.

Sound recordings
Sound recordings representing the social background and occupations of the community form a valuable part of the local studies library. Such recordings are particularly important when the sound is of interest in itself: for instance, dialect, folksong. Other recordings which can be especially useful are those recording working practices in local trades and industries, as well as living and social conditions of the interviewees.

In addition to sound recordings of the kind described above, commercially produced tapes and discs (e.g. of local choirs) should be acquired. Talking newspapers for the blind are now produced in many districts and should be acquired for collections.

Visual recordings
Film. Cinefilm has the advantage of permanence and is still the most desirable medium for conserving visual moving images. 16mm film is to be preferred where possible. *Warning*: There is a serious danger of

spontaneous combustion occurring in 35mm cinefilm made before 1951. If any such film is held it should be kept as cool as possible and professional advice sought concerning copying and destruction of the original.

Video. Although a medium rapidly expanding in use, video film is not of reliable permanence. Video recordings will form part of the stock of a local studies collection, but professional advice should be sought in regard to rare material with a view to having more permanent copies made on film when necessary. Rare material on film can be transferred on to video to increase its availability.

10 Archives

Authorities administering a service which includes archives should recognize that this implies a commitment in staff and accommodation so that fully satisfactory professional standards for archival storage and conservation can be achieved. If this commitment cannot be met, archive material should be deposited in the most appropriate archive repository available in which full archival care can be given.

Ideally, archive and library collections should be housed in one building as this is the most satisfactory arrangement for the user.

Many Local Studies Librarians in Scotland have been delegated to take responsibility for care of records of former local authorities, in cases where such records vest in their own authority, under the terms of the Local Government (Scotland) Act, 1973.

11 Conservation

The local studies collection usually includes a high proportion of material that is rare and in some cases unique. It is the duty of the Local Studies Librarian to give high priority to protecting the material from theft and from damage by unfavourable environments.

All Local Studies Librarians must have access to conservation facilities for the repair of books, maps and documents. If internal library conservation facilities are not available an outside firm of conservators should be employed: some library binderies have a conservation service available. Local record offices will often advise on conservation, and may in some cases be able to give practical help.

Local Studies Librarians should be familiar with currently recognized standards of storage (e.g. temperature, humidity) for all materials in their care, whether these are books, documents, or other forms such as tape and film. Care should be taken to protect books on library shelves from sunlight or other adverse conditions. Staff should be aware of guidelines and policy statements which have been issued by The Library Association or other relevant bodies.

In some cases it is necessary to use a microform or other copy instead of the original in order to avoid undue wear and tear. This may be requisite when the original form is badly deteriorated (e.g. some old newspapers) or is very rare. When a copy is made for this reason it should always be used instead of the original except in very special circumstances. Microfilm negatives should be stored in secure microfilm cabinets away from both the positive film and the original copies.

Photographic negatives should be stored separately

from prints, as a precaution against total loss of items in the collection in the event of a mishap.

12 Classification and cataloguing
A variety of classification schemes has been devised for use in local studies libraries, but none has yet been accepted as outstanding. Choice of a scheme should involve the consideration of as many schemes as possible, with special attention being paid to their relative performance in use, including computer compatibility.

Non-book materials may require a special classification scheme to be used.

Alternatively, provision of a detailed verbal subject index, giving multiple access to items, might be considered more appropriate than classification.

Cataloguing should be detailed, with adequate bibliographical descriptions.

Detailed analytical indexing should be a feature of library local studies catalogues.

13 Exploitation of collections
Contact with local groups can benefit both library and user. Whilst the main purpose of the exploitation of collections is to improve the use of the collections, all contacts made with local people and organizations can and should be used as an opportunity to acquire material for the library, e.g. club magazines; local photographs and postcards; school magazines.

Community groups. It is important to encourage and

develop close links with community groups of all kinds. The local studies library is in an excellent position to establish contact with such groups, as its staff are alert to the activities of the local community as a normal part of their work in acquiring a permanent record of the locality. The local studies library can encourage local groups by providing talks and exhibitions. Exhibition space for groups to display material should be made available where possible.

Education. Contact with schools, colleges, further education classes and other educational groups should be closely maintained. Positive steps should be taken to make teachers, lecturers and education advisers aware of available facilities, and local studies staff should be well-informed about modern methods of teaching local studies. Full liaison should be maintained with school library services, and the local studies library should be concerned to make material available for use in school project work, including the provision of reprographic copies of suitable items for classroom use.

The private researcher. The most valuable and permanent studies of the history of a locality are often produced by the individual enthusiast, who should be encouraged to make the results of his work available to the library, including unpublished essays and theses.

Occasionally a researcher will make demands on a local studies library which cannot reasonably be met. The task of the Local Studies Librarian is to provide the materials for research and to draw the attention of the researcher to groups of material which may be useful to him, both within and beyond the immediate collection. It is not incumbent on the librarian to undertake detailed research on behalf of the enquirer, although moderate requests for information should always be entertained, with special consideration being given to postal enquirers who are unable to visit the library because of distance or disability. It is the duty of the Local Studies Librarian to ensure that adequate guidelines are available to assist staff to make decisions in cases they may encounter.

The media. Radio, television and the local press usually recognize local studies topics as subjects of considerable public interest. Links with the media should be established and exploited to advertise services and encourage fuller use of collections.

Exhibitions. Exhibitions can provide (a) educational and community information, and (b) publicity for the local studies collection with a view to acquiring material. Opportunities to stage exhibitions of both kinds should be welcomed both within the library and at outside locations.

The standard of display should always be professional, if simple. The services of a library display officer should be employed if available. Care should be taken that all information imparted by a display is accurate.

14   Local service points

Community libraries have a vital role to play in establishing a close working relationship between the library service and its users. In the field of local studies a genuine rapport can be generated, with local residents playing an active part in the development and enjoyment of local studies collections. Carefully planned exhibitions of local material can result in the deep involvement of a community over a period of time, to a degree which only a local studies project can hope to achieve. Cooperation should be established with key members of a community, who can be effective in collecting material from residents present and past. The results of such collecting activity can then be displayed, with a further consolidation of interest in the library local collection.

The enthusiasm generated by activities such as those outlined above should be maintained by constant attention to local collections in branch libraries as well as in the main collections. Branch collections may consist partly of purchased material, and partly of materials gathered by the community. It is essential that the content of branch library collections is monitored by the local studies department to ensure a proper balance appropriate to the particular locality. Branch libraries require an adequate supply of titles relating to the local area, and will also find that such items as albums of local photographs or scrapbooks of cuttings are of considerable value. Original items received by donation at subsidiary service points should be forwarded to the local studies department for a decision about their permanent location. Mobile library services should not be overlooked as a useful link with rural communities.

It is particularly important in view of the role of community libraries that local library staff be given adequate training to familiarize them with the wide range of local studies material available, and staff should also be educated in the skills of involving the local community in local studies activities.

Attention should be paid to groups in the community who have special needs or play a special part in local life. For instance, reminiscence therapy for the elderly can be greatly assisted by the use of material copied from the local studies collection, while the traditions and customs of ethnic minorities should be recognized as part of the history of the area.

15 Income generation
Some aspects of local studies librarianship lend themselves to income generation: provision of genealogical research services and the publication and sale of such items as local calendars and greetings cards are examples of possible projects. While such projects may be acceptably developed for this purpose, it is essential that extra staff and accommodation are made available to ensure that the additional workload is not added to the existing duties of local studies staff.

If an income generating project such as the provision of a genealogical research service is planned, care must be taken to protect fully the existing free service to users who visit the library to undertake research in person. This free service should include personal help from staff to a degree comparable with assistance given to other users of the local studies service.

16 Publishing
Library publications bring into print worthwhile material which would not otherwise be available either because of the lack of suitable local publishers or because the material would not be a viable undertaking for a commercial publisher. New titles extend the range of knowledge available and are of primary importance in a publishing programme. It is recognized that the publication of local history material can be financially advantageous to a library service, but this should not be regarded as the main motive for publication.

The publication of postcards from the library's illustrations collection should be regarded as a valid activity, as it is a means of making such illustrations more widely available.

Publication of local studies material in a form designed for school use is a means of increasing the usefulness of a local collection in the classroom. Examination syllabuses increasingly require the use of local source material by students, with the attendant difficulties of damage by over use. Reproduction of material for teaching purposes is one way of alleviating this problem, as well as providing a constructive link between the teacher and the local studies library.

The implications of a publishing programme in terms of staff must be considered when the programme is being planned. Although staff may often be willing to help with preparation of the text, the commitment of staff time to the technical aspects of publication must be recognized by management when such work is undertaken.

No library should produce a book which falls below accepted standards of bibliographical competence (name of publisher, date, correct and adequate biblio-graphical information in references and bibliographies, etc.), and a planned house-style is helpful in the systematic maintenance of good standards of production. The use of acid-free paper is highly desirable when publishing local studies material.

The best possible author in a subject field should always be sought for a publication being initiated by the library. Authors should be paid a publication royalty or fee.

17 Equipment

Computers and their applications

Computers have opened up greater possibilities for exploiting local studies materials. Local Studies Librarians should take advantage of any computerization undertaken by the library service, or consider buying a microcomputer for their own library's use. Microcomputers continue to become more affordable, with increasing storage capacity, software packages offer more flexibility of application, and computer systems can be easy to use with a minimum of computing skill. They are attractive as a means of enhancing indexing provision, and for maintaining information files or holdings lists. Preparation of items for publication is facilitated by use of a word-processing package. The ability to search files more effectively and to display or print search results can give an improved service to readers and staff.

When participating in a large scale library computerization project, full attention should be given to the possibilities of a fully integrated scheme for cataloguing local studies collections in an area, including branch library collections and public collections in related institutions such as record offices and museums. Non-book material such as press cuttings, prints, architectural drawings, etc. may usefully be considered for inclusion in such a scheme. Print-out facilities will greatly enhance the use of such a catalogue as a bibliographical resource.

The Local Studies Librarian should be alert to advances in technology which may prove useful in local studies libraries and should also ensure that equipment already in use is replaced and updated as necessary.

Other equipment

Storage equipment. Care should be taken to acquire appropriate storage equipment for special material such as maps and microforms.

Microform readers. The quantity of material available in microform continues to increase. In addition to the extensive newspaper collections now held on micro-form, local record offices are increasingly involved in microfilming projects of which libraries may take advantage. Film of census enumerators' returns is now widely held by libraries and heavily used by geneal-ogists; genealogical research is also prompting acqui-sition of microform material such as the *International genealogical index* and the Office of Population Censuses and Surveys' index of births, marriages and deaths. It should be recognized that adequate microform readers and reader-printers must be provided for the use of this material: expenditure on the acquisition of the microform has often been considerable, and expenditure on the associated equipment should be accepted as necessary for its full exploitation.

Photocopiers. Photocopying equipment is now widely available and, carefully used, can save much wear and tear on original material. Copies should never be made, however, if this would cause damage to the original, e.g. because a volume is too heavy to lift comfortably, or if material would have to be bent or folded. Staff should always be made aware of the damage that careless photocopying can cause, should be given as much guidance as possible as to what can be copied safely, and should be supported in any decision to disallow the photocopying of material if it would be detrimental to the conservation of any item. All staff who photocopy material should also be given full guidance as to the restrictions of copyright legislation.

Photographic equipment. Unless the services of a library photographic department are available, a good single-lens reflex camera can be a very useful tool in a local studies library, both for copying photographs and for record photography, and should be provided whenever financial resources allow. Projectors for slides and film should be available to the Local Studies Librarian to enable exploitation of the collection.

Oral and video recorders. Equipment to play oral recordings and a tape recorder for use in oral history projects undertaken by the library should be available. Reel-to-reel recorders are still the best for oral recordings, but excellent cassette recorders are now available, and may be the only acceptable machines in many cases on grounds of cost. Expert help should always be sought when purchasing equipment for oral recording. Video recordings are becoming increasingly common, and access to a video machine will become necessary as soon as recordings are acquired.

18   Staff
Every public library authority should have a local studies department, with a specialist Local Studies Librarian in charge responsible for the supervision of local studies collections and services throughout all the libraries of the local authority. This post should be specifically designated as that of Local Studies Librarian. Supporting staff should be provided in sufficient numbers not only to answer day-to-day queries, but also to enable satisfactory standards of the acquisition, cataloguing and indexing of material to be maintained. In situations where local staff levels cannot accommodate a full-time Local Studies Librarian, the

Reference Librarian should be entrusted with oversight of the local studies service, which should be recognized as one of the most important and valid areas of reference work.

The Local Studies Librarian should have full professional qualifications, and should have either completed a course on local studies work as part of his/her qualifying examinations, or be able to demonstrate that he/she has attended other formal courses appropriate to his/her specialist duties as a Local Studies Librarian.

The Local Studies Librarian must maintain active links with relevant societies if the resources of the collection are to be fully publicized and exploited. It should be recognized that such societies invariably meet at evenings and weekends, and that the Local Studies Librarian will therefore be required to work some unsocial hours. Such work should be regarded as part of the normal duties of the Local Studies Librarian, and recompense in time or payment made accordingly. It should not be regarded as a spare time or voluntary activity, and the staffing consequences should be taken into consideration.

Adequate training in local studies provision should be given to all members of staff in central and branch libraries. Junior members of staff in their capacity as counter assistants are often the first point of contact between the user and the local studies library, and should have a general knowledge of the services which the local studies library can provide, the material (maps, directories, photographs etc.) which it contains, and related matters such as copyright law. Professional staff should have an even closer familiarity with the material. It is the duty of the Local Studies Librarian to ensure that adequate training and information are provided for the staff concerned.

The modern Local Studies Librarian must have the highest standard of professionalism, as the post requires the ability to organize an active department, in which care of rare material, oversight and guidance of staff, and service to a discerning clientele must be accompanied by a well-informed knowledge of the content of local studies material and the methods by which it is used. It is therefore essential that the post carries a salary grade that reflects its seniority, 'so that librarians who do not progress to higher posts of a more general character may be encouraged to become and remain specialists to the great advantage of the library service'.* It is important that the number of staff in the department is not an overriding factor in the consideration of a salary scale, as local studies departments are almost invariably smaller than those in other areas of library provision.

19 Accommodation

The physical location and construction of areas designed to house local studies collections should be carefully planned, and the opportunity taken to provide accommodation at fully satisfactory levels when buildings are constructed or adapted. Equipment should be installed to maintain the correct environmental conditions for rare material.

---

* *Standards of public library service in England and Wales*. Report of the Working Party appointed by the Minister of Education in March 1961 (Bourdillon Report), paragraph 93. (HMSO, 1962).

Areas designated as public study areas should contain adequate seating accommodation, with a generous provision of large tables on which maps, newspapers and other large items can be consulted with ease. Space should also be allocated for specialist equipment such as computer terminals, microform readers and printers. Adequate access and user facilities should be provided for disabled people.

Secure storage accommodation must be provided and should be immediately adjacent to the local studies library; provision should include suitable furniture (e.g. non-standard sizes of shelving, map cabinets, large format filing cabinets, a safe). Fire alarms should be installed, and fire escapes should be planned to avoid public egress through secure areas (through a closed store, for instance) or by routes which are not overseen by library staff. Adequate provision should be made in the storage accommodation for future expansion; this is always a matter of concern to local studies departments, as little material is withdrawn from stock. The position of the store within a building should also be matter of concern: basement stores, for instance, are unsuitable.

Open access to some of the printed material is of great advantage to the researcher, and the possibility of providing some open access accommodation should be considered when a department is planned. While it is not suggested that rare material should be put at risk, duplicate copies of some of the most useful material can often be purchased on the second-hand market, and collections of such items can be assembled for open access use. In some cases bound photocopies of rare volumes may be a means of supplementing the items available on open shelves.

20 Local Studies Centres

Convenience to the library user is of prime importance, and towards achieving this end the local studies library, the local museum and the archives department should be situated in close juxtaposition, with the staff of the three departments working in close cooperation. While present buildings in most cases preclude such proximity, it is an ideal which should be studied when new building complexes are planned. In such a situation joint collecting policies, shared exhibitions, services for schools and the general fusion of information and expertise can result in a local studies service of the highest order.

21 Copyright

The requirements of copyright legislation have been mentioned in some preceding sections. It is essential that expert advice is taken on such matters as copyright in commissioned photographs, authors' rights in works published by the library, copyright in unpublished materials and, very importantly, the procedures necessary to authorize multiple copies for classroom use as detailed in the Copyright, Designs and Patents Act, 1988 (which came into force on 1 August 1989).

FURTHER READING

Association of County Archivists, *Bringing archives closer to the public*, Alan Norton (ed.), University of Birmingham Institute of Local Government Studies (INLOGOV), 1988.

Baynes-Cope, A. D., *Caring for books and documents*, 2nd edition, British Library, 1989.

Cornish, Graham, *Copyright: interpreting the law in libraries and archives*. Library Association, 1990. ISBN 0 85365 709 2.

Dewe, Michael (ed.), *Manual of local studies librarianship*. Gower, 1987.

Dureau, J. M., *Principles for the preservation and conservation of library materials* by J. M. Dureau and D. W. G. Clements, (IFLA Professional reports, No. 8) International Federation of Library Associations and Institutions, 1986.

Great Britain. Statutes. *Copyright, designs and patents act, 1988.* HMSO, 1988.

Great Britain. *Statutory instruments*. S. I. 1989 No 1212: Copyright. *The copyright (librarians and archivists) (copying of copyright material) regulations 1989.*

Hobbs, J. L., *Local history and the library*, 2nd edition, completely revised and partly rewritten by G. A. Carter. Deutsch, 1973.

Library Association, *Preservation and conservation*, Policy statement, Library Association, 1987.

Makepeace, Chris E., *Ephemera: a book on its collection, conservation and use*. Gower, 1985.

Nichols, Harold, *Local studies librarianship*, Bingley, 1979.

Permanent paper, Library Association/National Preservation Office/Publishers' Association, 1986.

Statement of policy relating to archives. Museums Association/ Society of Archivists/Library Association, 1981.

Ratcliffe, F. W., *Preservation policies and conservation in British libraries: a report of the Cambridge University Library Conservation Project*, by F. W. Ratcliffe and D. Patterson. (Library and Information Research reports, No 25), British Library, 1984.